Stoicism

Leadership, Discipline, Mindset, Wisdom and Spiritual Exercises of the virtuous Stoic Ethics. Overcome Anxiety, Depression & Destructive Emotions and become the very best version of Yourself

By

Jimmie Powell

Table of Contents

Introduction 6
Chapter 1: What Is Stoicism? 11

    The Stoic Principles 14
    The Four Cardinal Virtues of Stoicism 16
    Social Philosophy 21
    Stoicism and Christianity 23
    Modern Usage of the Word Stoicism and Its Thoughts 25

Part 1: Disciplining Our Own Desires – Understanding What We Need and What We Want 29

Chapter 2: Learning What We Can Control 30

    Letting Go of Control in Our Lives 33
    What Am I Afraid Will Happen If I Do Decide to Let Go of the Control? 38
    Whose Business Are you In? 39
    Would Letting Go Feel Like I Was Gaining Freedom? 40
    How Do I Accept Things the Way They Are? 41

Chapter 3: How to Live in a Way That Meets with Nature 45

    Harmony with the Environment 46
    Harmony with the Community 47
    Harmony with Your Means 48

Harmony with Your Ability 49

Chapter 4: Material Possessions and How We Handle Them with Stoicism 51

External Things Aren't Going to Lead to Happiness ... 51

Most Things Are Not Worth the Care You Give Them. 53

The Amount of Items You Own Is in Your Control 54

Items Can Bring You Conditional Happiness, But They Don't Bring True Happiness 55

Essential Things Are Worth Your Focus 56

Material Possessions Aren't Bad; You Just Need to Think Them Through 58

Chapter 5: What Is the Spiritual Leaning of a Stoic 60

Serving God / the Logos 62

What Are You Serving and What Is the Highest Thing in Your Life at This Point? 63

Internal Service, Not an External Spectacle to Others. 64

Askesis 65

Serving the City of God Before Serving the City of Man 67

Part 2: How Do Stoics Behave in the World? 69

Chapter 6: The Importance of Virtue and Character 70

Chapter 7: Do I Need a Role Model to Be a Stoic? 79

How Can the Self-Distancing Help with Decision Making? 84

Chose a Role Model for Your Own Life 86

How I Put It All Together 88

Chapter 8: How Stoicism Can Help Deal with Mental Illness and Disability 91

How Stoicism Can Help with Depression and Anxiety 95

How Stoicism Can Help with Disabilities 99

Part 3: How to React to Things That Happen Around Us 104

Chapter 9: Stoics Views on Suicide and Death 105

Perception 106

Action 110

Will 112

Chapter 10: How to Deal with Negative Emotions 117

Chapter 11: Friendship and Love in a Stoic Life 126

Part 4: Spiritual Exercises to Become a Stoic 136

Chapter 12: The Best Exercises to Create a Stoic in You 137

Practice Misfortune 137

Train Your Perception to See Things Differently 139

Remember That Everything Is Ephemeral 140

Try to See Things from Above 141

Think About Your Own Mortality 142

Think About Whether the Situation Is in Your Control
.... 143
Spend Some Time Journaling 144
Practice Negative Visualization 145

Conclusion 147

© Copyright 2019 by __Jimmie Powell____ - All rights reserved.

The following eBook is reproduced below with the goal of providing information that is as accurate and reliable as possible. Regardless, purchasing this eBook can be seen as consent to the fact that both the publisher and the author of this book are in no way experts on the topics discussed within and that any recommendations or suggestions that are made herein are for entertainment purposes only. Professionals should be consulted as needed prior to undertaking any of the action endorsed herein.

This declaration is deemed fair and valid by both the American Bar Association and the Committee of Publishers Association and is legally binding throughout the United States.

Furthermore, the transmission, duplication, or reproduction of any of the following work including specific information will be considered an illegal act irrespective of if it is done electronically or in print. This extends to creating a secondary or tertiary copy of the work or a recorded copy and is only allowed with the express written consent from the Publisher. All additional rights reserved.

The information in the following pages is broadly considered a truthful and accurate account of facts and as such, any inattention, use, or misuse of the information in question by the reader will render any resulting actions solely under their purview. There are no scenarios in which the publisher or the original author of this work can be in any fashion deemed liable for any hardship or damages that may befall them after undertaking information described herein.

Additionally, the information in the following pages is intended only for informational purposes and should thus be thought of as universal. As befitting its nature, it is presented without assurance regarding its prolonged validity or interim quality. Trademarks that are mentioned are done without written consent and can in no way be considered an endorsement from the trademark holder.

Introduction

Congratulations on downloading *Stoicism*, and thank you for doing so!

The following chapters will discuss everything that you need to know to get started with the philosophy of Stoicism. There are a lot of people who have never even heard about Stoicism—and a lot of those who have heard about this school of thought and have misconceptions about it. They assume that in order to be a Stoic, they need to live a life that is void of emotions—one that means they can't have close relationships where they can't care about others and that they need to be able to ignore all of the emotions that come their way.

This is a big misconception that comes with Stoicism. Stoics are not void of any emotions that are out there. Rather, they are able to take a look at the different emotions that they are feeling, and then they decide whether those emotions are warranted in that situation or if they would like just brush it off and move on to another part of their day.

Rather than letting the emotions get the best of them, and rather than ruining relationships and losing control because of the emotions, a Stoic gets to be the one in control all of the time. The Stoic gets to choose when to show their emotions and when to just leave things alone. This can give them a benefit of more freedom and happiness in their own lives.

This guidebook is going to take some time to discuss Stoicism and all of the different parts that come with this school of thought. There is so much to love about Stoicism and all the ways that it is able to improve your life. It can help you be in control over your own life and your own emotions. It can help you look at death in a different manner. It can help you build up more friendships and love than before. Lastly, it can help with almost every aspect of your life—as long as you learn how to use it properly.

However, those are just a few of the ways that Stoicism can help your life. You can use it in so many ways—and still feel emotions like anyone else. This guidebook will also talk about the different ways that Stoicism can help you with issues like dealing with death, handling depression and anxiety, and just getting rid of some of the negative thoughts that may plague you now. We will even take a look at how Stoicism can work well with religion, such as how many major religions in the world share some basic tenants with Stoicism as well.

There is so much that comes with Stoicism. This is a school of thought that a lot of people just don't understand. Even though it comes from ancient times, it can work out so well in our modern world as well. When you are ready to learn more about Stoicism and how it can improve your own life, make sure to check out this guidebook to help you get started today.

There are plenty of books on this subject on the market—thanks again for choosing this one! Every effort was made to ensure it is full of as much useful information as possible. Please enjoy!

Chapter 1: What Is Stoicism?

Stoicism is a philosophy that was founded in Athens by Zeno in the 3rd century BC. However, there are many well-known Greeks who practiced this philosophy as well including Seneca, Epictetus, and Marcus Aurelius. This is a philosophy that asserts that virtue, like wisdom, is happiness—and that judgment should be based on the behavior of the person, rather than on their words. This ideology also talks about how we don't have any control over and can't rely on external events, but we can control ourselves and the way we respond to the world.

The ideology of Stoicism has just a few main teachings, which then helps keep things simple along the way. Stoicism is going to set out to help us remember how unpredictable the world can be. It helps us remember how brief a moment our life is. It shows us how to be strong and steadfast and how to keep in control of ourselves. Finally, it teaches that the source of the unhappiness that we feel lies in our impulsive dependency on our reflexive senses—rather than on any logic.

Stoicism isn't going to waste time with complicated theories about the world, but it is going to work to help us overcome any destructive emotions that may come up—and it teaches followers to let go of the things they can't control and *act* on the things that we *can* control. It is built more on taking action on the things that we can control—rather than just talking and debating about the world.

There are three main leaders that came up with the idea of Stoicism. Marcus Aurelius, the emperor of the Roman Empire at that time, sat down each day to write down notes for himself about humility, compassion, and restraint. Epictetus, who was a slave then went on to start his own school where he then taught many of the greatest minds of the Roman Empire, was a leader as well. Then, there was Seneca, who, when Nero decided to turn on him and demanded that he commit suicide, could only think of how he would comfort his friends and his wife.

Of course, it is not only these three individuals who practiced Stoicism. It has been practiced throughout the world by entrepreneurs, writers, artists, presidents, kings, and more. Both historical, as well as modern, men will decide to use Stoicism as a way of life to help them glean more happiness and avoid issues overall.

There are different principles that come with Stoicism, but the basic idea is that we need to learn to accept the things that are in our control and let go of anything that we can't control. There are many people who will choose to try and control everything. When something doesn't go their way or when they can't control the world, they get angry and upset and anxious overall.

However, this is a miserable way to live life. There are always going to be things in our lives that we wish we could control but can't—and getting upset and letting negative emotions take over can lead us to have a reaction that doesn't fit with the situation. While we can't control all of the situations and things that happen in our lives, we can have control over the way that we react and behave with these situations. Being able to do this is at the core of Stoicism and how it can benefit everyone.

The Stoic Principles

In our modern times, Stoic principles have been able to find their way into accepted popular wisdom, as goals that everyone should work to aspire to. There are a lot of different principles that come with Stoicism, but some of the main ideas that are part of the ethics of Stoic philosophies include:

- **Nature**: Nature is always rational, unlike some of the emotions that humans have.
- **Law of Reason**: Everything in the universe is going to be governed by the laws of reason. Man isn't able to escape its forces, but he can, in his own way, follow the law deliberately.
- **Virtue**: A life that can follow rational nature is one that is considered virtuous.

- **Wisdom**: Wisdom is going to be the main virtue when it comes to Stoicism. From here you will get the other virtues of Stoicism including justice, self-control, bravery, and insight.
- *Apatheia*: Since the passions that most people hold are going to be irrational, it is important that your life is a battle against these passions. Intense feelings are to be avoided.
- **Pleasure**: Pleasure is not seen as good or bad. This kind of pleasure can only be acceptable if it doesn't get in the way of your quest to reach virtue.
- **Evil**: Evil is all in the perception of the individual. Things like death, illness, and poverty are not seen as evil.
- **Duty**: Virtue is something that should be sought out, not just for pleasure, but for duty.

These principles are very important when it comes to being a Stoic. There are a lot of different ideas that come into play for those who want to live the life of a Stoic, and writing them all down and keeping track of them can sometimes seem overwhelming when you first get started. But following the basic Stoic principles that are above, you can keep all of it in check and see some great results with happiness and fulfillment with your life as a Stoic.

The Four Cardinal Virtues of Stoicism

With Stoicism, the cardinal virtues are going to be the four principal moral virtues that Stoics are meant to follow. All of the other virtues that you have in life are going to hinge on these four main ones. But the main virtues that you can use in your life when you are preparing to be a Stoic include temperance, fortitude, justice, and prudence.

These four virtues come up in Plato's Republic, and many of these entered into Christian teaching through Aristotle and other teachers through the years. Unlike some of the theological virtues, which are seen as the gifts of God through grace, these virtues are ones that anyone is able to practice. It doesn't matter if you are practicing Christianity, practicing Buddhism, or practicing some other religion.

This is why these four virtues are often seen as the foundation of morality.

The first virtue that we can look at is prudence. This one is ranked as the first one because it is concerned with the intellect of a person. Aristotle defined prudence as the right reason to practice and is the virtue that we want to use in order to judge, in the correct manner, what is right and what is wrong for the situation we are in. When we mistake something evil as something that is good, we are not using the virtue of prudence. In fact, in that scenario, we are actually showing our lack of prudence.

Prudence can be a hard one to develop and use. It is easy to fall into error in your life. This is why prudence is going to ask us to seek out the counsel of others, especially of those who we think to be sound judges of morality. If we decide to disregard the advice and the warnings of others who have a judgment that is different than ours, simply because their judgment is different, is a big sign of imprudence and shouldn't be done.

The next virtue that a Stoic must have is justice. This one is important because it is going to be connected with the will. Justice is a constant and a permanent determination to give everyone their rightful due in all situations. The idea that justice can be blind is perfect to a Stoic because it should be used no matter how we like the other person. If we owe that person a debt, then the Stoics say that we should repay exactly what is owed. And we must treat everyone in a fair and just manner at all times.

Justice is going to be connected to the idea of rights. Too many times we will use justice as an idea that is negative, such as "They got what they deserved". But justice, when it is used in the proper manner, is supposed to be a positive thing. Injustice is going to occur when we as individuals, or through the help of the law, deprive someone of what they are owed. It is important to remember that to the Stoics, legal rights should never be more important than the natural rights of all people.

The third virtue that we are going to take a look at is known as fortitude. This one can often be known as courage as well, but it is important to know that the idea of courage is going to be different than how we imagine it in our modern society. Fortitude is going to make it easier for us to overcome any fears that we have, and to remain as steady as possible in our will when obstacles get in our way during life.

Fortitude or courage is always going to be reasonable and reasoned. The person who uses it doesn't seek out danger just because the danger is there. Prudence and justice are the virtues where someone will decide what they need to do. Fortitude and courage will give us the strength to get these things done. It doesn't mean that we go looking for trouble, but it does mean that we get the courage to keep working towards our goals and never quitting.

And then there is the fourth virtue of temperance. While fortitude is going to concern itself with the restraint of fear so that we are able to act, temperance is going to be the restraint of our desires or our passions. For example, food, drink, housing and more, are necessary for our survival, both as an individual and as a species as a whole. But having a disordered desire for these goods can be really disastrous for our physical and moral lives.

Temperance is a virtue that will help us to stay away from excess. Because of this, it is going to require us to be able to balance out goods that are legitimate and necessary against our inordinate desire for these. The legitimate use of these goods can be changed based on the times of our lives. But it is important that we know how to properly use these goods, and when to stop, in order to practice temperance in our lives.

All of these virtues are going to work together. In the views of the Stoic, you can't be virtuous if you only have one of these virtues in your life, and if any of the virtues are missing, then you wouldn't be considered virtuous either. It is important that you work on improving all of these aspects in your life, in order to truly see virtuousness in your own life.

Social Philosophy

One distinctive feature that comes with Stoicism is the idea of cosmopolitanism. With this idea, all people are going to be manifestations of the same universal spirit. There are no tribes or countries when it comes to Stoicism. Instead, it is all about following brotherly love and working to help out each other, regardless of race and where you are from. Epictetus comments on the relationship that man should have with the world. According to him, each human is primarily going to be a citizen of their own commonwealth—but a man needs to remember that they are also a member of the great city of gods and men, and here the city politics is just going to be a copy. We are citizens of the world before we are citizens of the country we live in.

In addition, most Stoics held that the external differences of people in terms of wealth and rank don't really matter when it comes to social relationships. Remember that many

Stoics came from varying backgrounds, including those who were rich and noble, all the way down to those who were slaves. Instead, Stoicism advocated that there should be a brotherhood of humanity and that all humans should be considered equal.

Due to all of these thoughts, Stoicism soon became the most influential school of thought in the Greco-Roan world, and there were many people who were interested in writing about and talking about this philosophy overall. Some of the most notable Stoics and the ones who help contribute to this ideology quite a bit during that time include Epictetus and Cato the Younger.

In particular, the Stoics were seen as different than others of the time because they urged that there should be more clemency towards the slaves. They wanted owners to remember that they, and the slaves, came from the same stock and lived on the same earth and that when each of them died, they would then be on the same terms again. Because of this, Stoics expected that the owner would treat the slave in a just and kind manner.

Stoicism and Christianity

As we will explore a bit more as we go through this guidebook, Stoicism, and Christianity—among other world religions—share a lot of similarities overall. While many of the founders of the church see Stoicism as more of a pagan philosophy and one that the followers should stay away from, you can quickly find that a lot of the ideas that are found in Christianity are similar to what is found in Stoicism as well.

Both of these ideologies assert that there should be inner freedom when it comes to facing the external world and all there is out there. Both of them talk about having a kinship with all other humans in the world. They talk about the temporary nature of the world and material possessions and our attachments. They ask followers to work towards a common goal of finding inner freedom under their own control, rather than searching around for material items to find that happiness and freedom.

As you are reading through this guidebook, you will find that there are a lot of similarities that show up between early Christianity, and the Christianity that many people follow today, and the Stoics. In fact, it is easy to practice both of them together in order to become a more virtuous person and to gain the happiness and freedom that you desire.

Even though the founders of many Christian religions would have never thought of themselves like the Stoics, and many may have even talked about the paganism of Stoicism, there are many similarities and both of these ideologies are based on the same kind of thoughts and virtues. We will explore this a bit later in more detail in this guidebook, but these two philosophies share some striking similarities, which makes them perfect for putting together and for helping a person live a virtuous life.

Modern Usage of the Word Stoicism and Its Thoughts

Even in our modern times, it is possible to utilize Stoicism to make our lives easier and happier. While the modern version of the word Stoicism has changed quite a bit, and it now means someone who has an indifference to joy, grief, pleasure, or pain, that is not how you would use the word in order to make your life a little better.

In reality, you can take the ideas of Stoicism and use them to make your life better. While many people have a misconception about what this Stoicism is about and how they can use it in their own lives, it can help you become more in control over the emotions and the situations that you are in right now. A Stoic person isn't someone who doesn't have any feelings. They do have feelings, and they do care about what is happening to other people. The difference is they get to decide when an emotion comes out and when to hide that emotion because it doesn't suit their needs.

How many times in your life have you gotten into a fight with someone else, or you have gotten mad at someone over something that was small. It may have been a little skirmish, nothing that was a big deal. But because the emotions started to get in control and take over, things quickly escalated and before you knew it, both of you were doing and saying things that you didn't mean and felt bad about later on.

In Stoicism, this kind of situation is less likely to happen. You get to be the one who is in charge of your emotions. This isn't to say that you don't have emotions at all, but rather, it is more about learning how to control the emotions that you have in order to improve your life.

The next time you are in one of these fights, and you start to feel anger coming up, you can take a step back. Is the situation really that bad that you need to start overreacting and getting mad? Sure they may have said something that was a little mean, but is that really a big deal and going to mess with your whole day? Could you find another way to deal with that situation, a way that isn't going to result in a big fight, hurt feelings, and lots of regrets when the anger has finally gone away?

This is where Stoicism gets to come into play. You are still going to feel the same emotions as before, but you get to be the one in control over that emotion, rather than letting the emotions take control over all these different situations in your own life. And this can do so much for you when it comes to living in the modern world.

When following Stoicism and gaining control over the things that you have some control over, such as your emotions, and letting go of the things you can't do anything about, you are slowly working to improve your overall life. You get the benefit of being in stronger and better relationships. You get the benefit of not letting so much of our modern world stress you out. You get the benefit of being happier and enjoying your life way more than you did in the past. There are just so many benefits that come from adding Stoicism to your life, even in our modern world.

Part 1: Disciplining Our Own Desires – Understanding What We Need and What We Want

Chapter 2: Learning What We Can Control

One of the main aspects that you need to work on when you are ready to start with Stoicism is learning what you can control and letting go of anything that you can't control. Many of the troubles that you run into in life come from the fact that you think you can control everything and then getting mad or upset about the fact that things don't go the way that you want.

There are always things in life that we aren't able to control. We can't control how people are going to react. We can't control if someone is going to get a promotion over us. We can't control how the traffic is going to work, how the weather is going to behave that day, and more. Letting your emotions take control when these things happen can lead to disaster.

How many times has something occurred in your life and then you lost your cool? You exploded and said things to someone that you later regretted? Did you feel that your anger started to boil up because you weren't able to control a situation that was going on around you? Once the anger or frustration or sadness or any other emotion starts to come up, you found that it was just going to get worse, and you would do whatever the emotion led you to.

The problem here is that while you can't control the situation that brought up the negative emotion, you can control the emotion itself. Yes, there will be times when the negative emotions come out after a situation. Even as a Stoic you are going to have emotions at some point. There is just no way around this. But whether or not you allow the emotions to come out and display themselves is completely in your control.

Let's say that someone says something mean to you. You start to feel angry. As a non-Stoic, you let the anger come out. You feel insulted and can't believe that someone would be so mean to you. You may start to yell at them, scream, and even hit at them until the tantrum gets out of control and you do and say things that you didn't mean and that you are ashamed of later on. In this scenario, your emotions have gotten control over you and getting them to calm down can be almost impossible.

As a Stoic, you would handle this situation in a slightly different manner. You can't control that the other person said the mean things to you. But you can control how you react. When the anger starts to come up, you can take a step back and think it through. Did that person really say something so mean? Does the situation really warrant you to get mad and overreact, or could you just walk away and move on with your day? Do you feel like putting that much energy into it at all? Even if the thing the other person said was really mean and hurtful, maybe they were having a bad day, and you getting angry and losing it will just make the situation worse.

You can see the differences between the two situations. In one, you lost your cool and did and said a lot of things that you are not at all that proud of now. But in the second situation, you were able to understand where the other person was coming from, and you were able to choose to walk away. Which method do you think will help you be happier, and to have more meaningful relationships in your life?

There are times when you will let those emotions out. You don't have to be emotionless in order to be a Stoic. The difference is that you get to control how much those emotions actually come out and play a part in your day. If you look at the situation and decide that the emotion is warranted in that case, then it is just fine to let it out. But the difference is that you get to be in control of the emotion, rather than letting the emotion be in control over you.

Letting Go of Control in Our Lives

How many times in your life do you deal with anger or anxiety? Even if it is not something that has been diagnosed as a problem in your life, it is still something that a lot of people deal with on a daily basis. They are anxious when things go against their plan, they get anxious when they get in a situation they are not able to control, and when this anxiety starts to come around, they feel anger at the same time.

Often our anger and our frustration are going to come from the fact that we think we need to be in control over everything. And when we naturally aren't able to change the circumstances and we can't change what is going on around us, we naturally start to feel a bunch of negative emotions around us, such as being overwhelmed, or sadness, frustration and anxious.

There are always going to be things out there that we can't control. And it doesn't matter how much we try to control those things, they are going to happen a certain way. Letting go of that control and letting things happen, and learning what you can actually control in your life is the key to ensuring that you live a happy life.

There are three things that we have to know when it comes to trying to control things. First, we like to try to be in control of things mostly because of what we think might happen in that situation if we don't. We have a fear of not being in control. If we don't plan things out and work towards controlling a situation, what might end up happening? The fear of the unknown forces us to try to control things that we really can't.

Another issue with control is that it is a result of being attached to a certain outcome. This outcome is often one that we think is the best for us. But this is making the assumption that we always know what is best for us, even though we don't. When we take the time to learn that we will be fine, no matter what happens during that situation, we learn that it isn't necessary to micro-manage the universe. We figure out how to let things go. And as soon as you learn to let things go, you open up the door to a ton of great possibilities, many of which were not there when you were too focused on managing and controlling the situations around you.

You will also find that the energy you put into surrendering and not worrying about controlling everything can accomplish a lot more than the energy you put into control.

The energy for control is going to be a bit different for everyone, but for a lot of people, it can include the vision getting narrowed down and focused, the breath getting more shallow, the adrenaline starts to pump more, and the rate of the heart increases.

Then the mind starts to move very quickly, going from one topic to another, going from the past to the future. It is hard to concentrate during this time because our minds are moving so quickly. There are also issues with poor memory and there isn't much present time awareness in this individual.

But things are a bit different when it comes to surrendering mode. During this kind of mode, it is easier to be calm and peaceful. Breathing deeply is easier and you will be able to see what is going on in the present moment. Your vision will extend around more so that you can see the bigger picture, and so much more. You can see why it is much better to have energy towards surrender rather than energy towards control.

And that is why it is so important to learn the art of surrender. Surrender literally means that you give up fighting. You stop with the fight against yourself. You stop with the fight against the natural flow of the universe. And you stop with the fight against reality. Surrender equals the complete acceptance of what is going to happen, or what is already there added with the faith that all is going to be well, even without my own input coming to play.

Of course, this is not always about inaction. It is more about taking the right actions from a place of surrender energy. For example, when you start to see that you are in control mode, stop and think of yourself as a small boat which is trying to go upstream against the current. This ends up being a real hard fight if the little boat keeps trying to go upstream. But this is what we are doing when we continue to try and control what is going on around us.

Now, visualize what it would be like to be in surrender mode. Imagine that the boat turned around, just floating downstream, and you get to just drop the oars. You are being pulled along gently, no effort is really needed from you. Isn't this a much easier type of scenario, one that lets you relax and enjoy what is going on in life, rather than working hard and feeling exhausted at the end.

There will be times when it is hard to make that shift, going from control to surrender. We know that it is a much better idea for us, but we often struggle to make the changes. Some of the things that you should ask yourself to see if it makes the process a bit easier includes:

What Am I Afraid Will Happen If I Do Decide to Let Go of the Control?

Often we decide to hold onto the control and refuse to let it go because we are scared of what would happen if we did let go of some of the control in our lives. Taking the time to pinpoint our actual fear, you can then question the validity of that fear. Is it true? Is that worst case scenario really going to happen if we don't hold onto control?

For example, let's say that you are worried that the night is going to be over and everything is ruined if your boyfriend doesn't pick up the eggplant on the way home from work, and you have already taken the time to remind him a bunch of times to do it, it is time to stop and question that assumption. Is your night really going to be ruined because one vegetable was left at the store? And even if it is ruined by your definition, what is really such a big deal about that? Often, the things that we let get to us are not that big of a deal. If your boyfriend forges the eggplant, just make the dish without it, pick a different dish to make, or consider going out and having a fun night together. Making things into the worst case scenario, when they really shouldn't be, is just making you miserable in the process.

Whose Business Are you In?

Things that are your business are the things that you can have a direct influence on. Are you there—or are you butting into someone else's business along the way? Often when we find that we are trying to control things that are outside of our own business, things don't go as smoothly as we would like. Others react in a negative way and get mad. You do not need to be in the business of other people. Let them handle their own business. This can help you reduce the amount of stress that you are dealing with, and can help strengthen more of your relationships because people won't feel like you are getting in the way as much.

Would Letting Go Feel Like I Was Gaining Freedom?

This is something that most of us aren't even going to consider when we are dealing with things in our lives. We assume that we have to keep control over everything. If we don't, we feel that things are going to fall apart on us. But really, how would you feel if you were able to let go of even one thing on that big list of yours? Would this lead to more time to spend with your family? Would it relieve some of the stress that you feel on a daily basis? What would that kind of freedom mean to you?

How Do I Accept Things the Way They Are?

There are several ways that you can make sure that you learn how to accept the things that you can control, and let go of the things that you can't control. These include:

- Learn how to be involved fully in the things that you do. Whichever task you are doing right now, put all of your thought and effort into it. This is going to help you center yourself and can keep all of those negative, and even outrageous thoughts, away from your mind. This can keep you to stay positive and do well overall.

- Learn to not control everything around you. No matter how much you try, you are not the one in control of everything. This is hard for some people to accept, but the sooner you do, the sooner you will be able to enjoy true happiness. The only thing that you can be in control of is your own actions and thoughts, and the rest you just have to let go of.

- Look at the bigger picture: When you get too focused on one situation, it is hard to think things through and look at the big picture. When you are in a situation, ask yourself if any of this will really matter in the future. Most things are not going to matter to you in a month or in a year, so why let them bother you so much now?
- Always be kind to others: Of course, being kind to yourself falls into this as well. Sometimes a lot of the negative that we push out into the world is caused by our own insecurities rather than by anything that others are doing to us. Learning how to treat ourselves the right way, as well as how to be kind to others, can make a difference in your life.
- Accept the things around you: It is important in this to learn how to accept others, to accept yourself, and accept that the only true way that we can leave a footprint in the world is when we learn how to impact, as well as change, the lives of others for the better. Learning to accept who we are, and not being

judgmental of others, can really lead to more happiness, and fewer negative thoughts, than before.

There are some things in life that we can control. But there are much more things in our lives that we really have no control over at all. Understanding what falls into each category can help you learn how to add more happiness to your life. Sometimes the best way to live our best life is to let go of the things that we can't control and not worry about them. While this can be hard, it does offer a lot of freedom overall.

This is probably one of the hardest parts of implementing Stoicism in your life. It is hard to let go of our control over things. But often, we don't really have that much control over things in the first place. We have just tricked ourselves into thinking that we have control, and then we get frustrated when we don't actually have that control.

Rather than letting our emotions get in the way and make us unhappy and letting those emotions get in the way of our happiness, it is time to learn how to just let go. It will do so much good for everyone, but especially for you. It may be hard, but the principles of Stoicism will help this become a reality in no time.

Chapter 3: How to Live in a Way That Meets with Nature

Part of working on a virtuous life as a Stoic is to make sure that you live in accordance with nature. Just like the hand is a part of the arm and that is a part of the body, we are a part of the whole society, and we need to be able to live our roll. Many times, our modern society works in a way that is the opposite of this idea. It thinks that you need to consume more and just live for your own wants and needs—without any consideration for anyone else. However, with Stoicism, this idea needs to be turned around a bit.

When it comes to the idea of living in accordance with nature, there are a few things that are going to come to mind. First, it means that you need to live in harmony with the environment that is all around you. It also means that you should live in harmony with your community, with your own means, and with your abilities. Let's take a look at each of these points and how they are going to work together to help you live in a way that meets up with nature and helps you be a Stoic.

Harmony with the Environment

The first place in our life where we need to have some harmony is the environment. The environment that we are talking about here is going to include both the social and the physical environments. You should try to live in harmony and keep balance, in these environments as much as possible. You should also be respectful and good to nature as much as possible.

A good example to look at when working on this is the idea of camping. When you are working with and interacting with the environment at all, think of it as a campsite when you are out camping. You want to make sure that when you leave the area, the campsite is in better condition compared to what it was when you got there. Your environmental and social environments need to always be left in better condition than when you first got there in order to live in harmony with all the different environments that go on in your life.

Harmony with the Community

When it comes to having harmony with your community, it is important for you to fit in as much as you can without compromising your own values. A part of being happy is having some kind of engagement with your community. When you do this, there is going to be less friction if you are able to maintain good relationships with those around you. As a Stoic, you will learn how to maintain these healthy relationships. You will be respectful of those around you. You will understand that everyone is a bit different and that each person has the right to behave the way that they want. It is best to not pass judgment on others. You don't necessarily know what they are going through, and your judgments may hinder some strong relationships with these individuals.

Harmony with Your Means

As a Stoic, it is important to live within your means. Don't allow yourself to get into a ton of debt in order to try to increase your quality of life, or to enjoy a lot of luxuries that you can't afford. It is much better for you to put your focus on improving the situation and control your spending as much as possible. Eventually, with some hard work and dedication, you will find that you can make your money work for you, and you may even be able to have more than you need in the end.

It doesn't matter how much money you earn, if you learn how to live within your means, you are going to have plenty. You will be able to pay your bills, get your debts paid off, and so much more. And if you work with devoting yourself to things that are actually important to you, rather than just on junk, you will have a full life without having to worry about making a ton more money.

You have to choose how to add in some more harmony with your means. This could include paying off your bills. It may include figuring out where you can cut things out of your budget. It may include starting a brand new budget and seeing how that can help you control your money. But no matter which way you do this, you need to make sure that you are the one in control over any money that you earn and that you spend.

Harmony with Your Ability

It is normal for most people to analyze themselves occasionly in order to determine your abilities or your talents, and then work to build up the skills that are necessary to support these. Each person has their own natural ability. Some people are good at visual fields. Some are good at math and sciences. Some can do well with athletics and others can write or sew, or make great recipes overall. Each of us is unique and will have our own natural abilities compared to others around us.

One thing that you have to consider with this is that it is important to separate your ability from your skill. Skills are things that can be learned, while abilities are more about the things that you were born with. This is a great thing to consider though. Even if you weren't born with the abilities to do some things, you can easily have the time to learn the skills to do those things, if you put your mind to it.

Natural ability and the talent that come with it can be an indication of some grand plan or something from the fates, or it could just be coincident in your life. But learning to accept the abilities that you are given, and embracing them and using them in a way that helps out others, can be the key to true happiness. Many times we are mad that we don't have other abilities or that we think our abilities just aren't worth our time. Accepting your own abilities and learning how to use them can make a difference in your life and can drop a lot of conflict at the same time.

Chapter 4: Material Possessions and How We Handle Them with Stoicism

In this chapter, we are going to take a look at how Stoicism views material possessions and if there is a limit on how many you can possess while still being considered a Stoic at the same time. This chapter will take some time to explore this issue a bit further and talk about how possessions are just fine with the ideology of Stoicism—as long as they are being used in a way to bring you a lot of happiness.

External Things Aren't Going to Lead to Happiness

Our modern society often goes in the opposite direction of Stoicism. The modern world always talks about how to get more wealth and get more things, and how to keep accumulating all those material possessions that just take up more space in our homes. With the idea of Stoicism though, you start to learn that wealth and fame are not going to be able to cure all of your problems, and these two things are not going to help make you happy. The real goodness in life is not found through wealth—but it is found through self-discipline, courage, justice, and even from wisdom.

It is more about the actions that make you happy. The really good is simple, and your actual needs are going to be pretty small and pretty cheap. While it is nice to have some material possessions and a bit of wealth, these things are not going to fix any of the internal issues that you are dealing with. Of course, this doesn't mean that having wealth is automatically going to lead to fear and more problems. The idea here is that if you are chasing wealth in order to make yourself happier, you are going to fail. But there are plenty of wealthy individuals who also successfully practice Stoicism as well. It is all in how you see the world and manage things.

Most Things Are Not Worth the Care You Give Them

Most of the things that you give your attention to are not really worth it. You don't need to try and keep up with everything that is happening out in the world. With how the media runs all the time, you wouldn't be able to keep up with it all even if you tried. While the media and others may broadcast everything as super important, most of it isn't worth our time. And it also doesn't matter that much if we know these things all the time anyway. Think about it, if the news item was really that important, we would probably hear about it from someone else anyway.

What this means is that most Stoics decide to cut out a lot of their news intake, and many of them do a drastic cut to their social media consumption. This provides them with more time, more energy, and more brainpower for the things that they find really important. You can concentrate on the things and the news items that are really important to you and your family, and cut out all the rest.

As a Stoic, you will develop a minimalist approach to media consumption. This can be beneficial because we all know that not every headline we see is really that important. The Stoic understands that it is fine to say "I don't know" or "I don't care" when it comes to some news items, rather than trying to keep up with all of it all the time.

The Amount of Items You Own Is in Your Control

As a Stoic, you will come to find that the number of items that you own is completely within your control. You do not have to go out and purchase all the brand new stuff that comes out in the advertisements and you don't have to try and keep up with the Joneses either. You are the one in control of how many items come into your home.

Once you realize that you have this kind of control, it can bring you a lot of freedom. You can walk into the store and only purchase the items that you need. You can say no to things and walk away without feeling guilty or bad. You get to decide what comes in and what goes out. And this can really help you enjoy more of the things that you want (when you have more money from not buying items and more free time from not cleaning those items up all the time, you can do more of what you want), you can gain true freedom and happiness in your life.

Items Can Bring You Conditional Happiness, But They Don't Bring True Happiness

Do you often find yourself longing for something that you don't have? This is something that is very typical in our society. We are always thinking "We'll be happy when..." fill in the blank with whatever answer you have there. We always put our happiness on hold to the future, and it is always conditional. We can't be happy right now because we can only be happy if or when something else happens.

Stoics knew that this kind of yearning, this always wanting more and better and in the future, is a big enemy when it comes to our freedom and our happiness. The more we start to desire things, and the more we need to do to acquire those things, the less we are actually going to enjoy our lives. When this happens, we aren't living to live. We are living just to get to the future, and we miss out on a lot of the great things that we have in our lives right now.

A modern Stoic is going to find this yearning and then chooses to ignore it. This doesn't mean that they choose to dismiss it and not even pay attention to it. That yearning is still there for the Stoic. But they choose to live in the present moment and enjoy their lives, rather than worrying about what is going to happen in the future so much.

Essential Things Are Worth Your Focus

For this one, start out by asking yourself what you find as the most important thing in your life. When we know what these things are from the beginning, it is easier to prioritize and then focus on those important things. You may have a cloudy vision about what you find as important, and this can lead to a lot of side roads that don't bring you any happiness. But when you really sit down and think about what you find as important, you will find that you start to bring more of that into your daily life.

Just like everyone else, you are given 24 hours in your day. You are the one who has to decide how you would like to spend that time. If you waste it away on things that are superficial, or on things that you don't really care about, then this can leave you feeling drained and tired at the end of the day. Yes, there are going to be some obligations that you just have to get through each day. But it is best if you are able to keep these down to a minimum as much as possible. Then, with the remainder of your time, you can focus on the things that you find really important.

Material Possessions Aren't Bad; You Just Need to Think Them Through

When you are a Stoic, it is just fine to have material possessions. Stoics do not live under bridges and own nothing. The issue isn't necessarily the material possessions that you own, it is how you use them. Learning how to use them in the proper manner, and being smart with the items that you do have, is the biggest difference between how a Stoic handles their things, and how other people will do this.

If you are purchasing items just to keep up with others and to keep up in the modern world, then it is time to stop. You aren't using these items to bring you happiness, and if you are influenced by commercials and other advertising, then you are not logically thinking about the purchases you are making.

Many Stoics find that practicing the ideas of minimalism can do wonders for them. This helps them start thinking through every item they own, and every item they decide to purchase in the future. They determine whether that item actually brings them happiness, if that item is something they would actually use, or if that item actually has some value for them.

If an item meets these requirements, then the Stoic, or the minimalist, will agree to keep it. If the item doesn't meet these requirements, then it is disposed of. In the case of not owning the item yet, if you don't find value in it, then you leave it on the shelf.

With material possessions, it is all about figuring out what you hold valuable, and what you are going to actually use. When you become a Stoic, you are not required to dump all of your items and live like a pauper in order to find happiness. But you do need to learn how to pick out items logically. Don't be influenced by what's on television, don't look at commercials, and don't just let your friends tell you what to purchase. You have to think through every purchase logically as a Stoic to ensure that you are making the right decisions for your happiness.

Chapter 5: What Is the Spiritual Leaning of a Stoic

When it comes to Stoicism, many wonder if this kind of ideology ever had a God that was followed. Did the ancient Stoics believe in a higher power, or did they become some of the earliest atheists? There is some debate about whether a Stoic actually follows a religion or not—and there are good points on either side of the debate.

To start, Stoicism is an ideology about how to live a happy life. It is a way for humans to let go of some of the things that they can't control and learn how to reign in some of the things that they do have control over. It doesn't really have its own religion attached to it, meaning that the individual can choose whether they want to implement this in with a religion that they already practice.

As we will discuss shortly, there are many similarities to the ideas that are found in Stoicism and in Christianity. In fact, many Christian religions will use a lot of the ideas that come from Stoicism to help them lead a good life. But it is possible to be a Stoic without following a set religion. And it is even possible to follow Stoicism while following some of the other religions that are out there.

This is part of the beauty of Stoicism. It teaches us how to become good people, and how to live a life that is simple and full of happiness. But it is adapted in a way that works for everyone. This was an ideology that started with the ancient Greeks, one that encompassed emperors, slaves, and everyone in between. This ideology has also grown and changed throughout history, helping to form early Christianity and is even found in our modern society.

Because of that, this is an all-inclusive type of philosophy. Whether you are a Christian, an atheist, a Buddhist or some other religion, you are going to find things that speak to you when it comes to being Stoic. With that said, we are now going to take a look at similarities between Stoicism and Christianity because these two ideas often go hand in hand.

Serving God / the Logos

One of the main similarities that you can find between Stoicism and Christianity is the idea of serving the will of God. Neither of these two philosophies demands that God, or in some cases more than one god, do your will. Many ancient Greeks would go out and ask the gods for more children, for a good harvest, for a good hunt and more. But Stoicism and Christianity were different in that they wanted the individual to do God's will. You needed to accept the will of God and try to serve it.

Here we should note that the Stoics were monotheists. They followed Heraclitus at the time and believed in one Logos. This is how they first became compared to the early Judaism, particularly that of Moses around two centuries before. Later Christians would draw on the idea of Logos, especially with the beginning of the Gospel of St. John. Some even argue that Stoicism was more monotheistic compared to Christianity because there were just Logos—without any angels, demons, Trinity, and Enemy.

What Are You Serving and What Is the Highest Thing in Your Life at This Point?

Another important thing that you will see with both of these ideologies is the question about what is the most important thing in your life and what do you serve. Who is your master and your God? Because everything in these two ideas is going to follow from there. There is an idea that is kind of similar when it comes to Plato, if you make public approval of your God, then you will make yourself a slave of the public, and then it is necessary to dance to their tune.

How does this work? If you decide to make money for your god, then you have to dance to that tune. You will have to bend and twist to that master. And money is not a very giving master when compared to the higher power of God. As either a Stoic or a Christian, it is important to figure out who that master is for you. Letting go of public opinions of you, and working towards a higher purpose can be the best way to make this happen.

Before you get started with either Christianity or with Stoicism, you need to know exactly who or what you are serving. Many people in our modern society are serving a master that is not God, and this has led them to a lot of unhappiness overall. They may be serving others, serving money and greed, or serving something else. When they turn their focus to serving God, or one deity that is similar to God, they are going to find a lot more purpose in their lives, a lot more freedom throughout their lives, and a lot more happiness as well.

Internal Service, Not an External Spectacle to Others

Both Christianity and Stoicism follow the idea of not portraying ostentatious worship of God. When you do this, you may be focusing your energy on showing off more for other people, rather than actually doing the worship. And this can taint it a little bit. Many Christian texts talk about praying and fasting in silence, so that you can get the attention of God, without worrying about getting any attention from men.

In addition, the Stoics felt the same way. According to Epictetus "when you are thirsty, take a little water in your mouth, spit it out, and tell no one." This goes along the same idea of serving your God or your master in silence. This doesn't mean that you can't share the news with others who are interested in learning, but it does mean that you shouldn't try to show off and impress others with what you are doing. This takes the sincerity out of the action and means you may as well not even do it at all.

Askesis

Early Christians would also follow the idea of the Stoics where the spiritual life would involve a few different parts. It would need to have some training of the mind, some training of the passions, and some training of the body. In fact, the desert fathers used these ideas to come up with a really rigorous program of mental and physical self-discipline.

In many parts of Orthodox Christianity, this kind of idea is still very much present. But there are some forms of Christianity that seem to have thrown this kind of idea out, such as with modern Evangelicalism. These groups seem to have gone away from training the passions, training the mind, and training the body in favor of being loud and having slightly soupy declarations for how much they love Jesus.

Overall, most Christians follow the idea of the Stoics in that they need to train their mind, body, and passions in order to see results with serving their master, and in improving their overall happiness. There seems to be some groups that are not quite as on board with this within the Christian group, but most of them will still follow this older idea that comes from the Stoics.

Serving the City of God Before Serving the City of Man

Early Christians have also followed the idea of Cosmopolis from the Stoics. The Cosmopolis is the City of God, and it is the idea that all good people should try to serve the City of God first and then they can serve their own tribe or area second. This is actually a radical idea, both when it was started and today, because it breaks through a lot of the racial and tribal barriers that humans have put in place and it insists that every person in the world shares a divine nature. If it were followed well, it would lead us to get along with one another better, rather than putting up all of the divides against each other.

While the ideas of Stoicism can work for everyone, regardless of what kind of religion they like to follow, it has a lot of similarities to what we find with ancient and modern Christianity. There is the idea of one God or one deity. There is the idea of training your mind, body, and passions to behave in a certain way. There are even the ideas that you need to do your praying or practice in private, rather than out in public, and you need to serve the city of God before worrying about your own little tribe.

There are certainly some differences between Stoicism and Christianity, which is why these two ideas haven't been lumped into just one group. But the similarities are pretty striking and it is no wonder that many Christian religions, as well as many Christians, will implement the Stoic principles into their lives in order to help them live a life that aligns more with their beliefs.

Part 2: How Do Stoics Behave in the World?

Chapter 6: The Importance of Virtue and Character

The Stoics decided to adopt the classification from Socrates of four aspects of virtue, which they thought of as four tightly interlinked character traits. These included wisdom, courage, temperance, and justice. To start with is wisdom. This practical wisdom is going to allow us to make decisions—ones that are going to improve our ethically good life. Courage has the option to be physical, but it more broadly refers to the moral aspect—or the courage to act well even when you are in a circumstance that is challenging.

Next is temperance—this is what will make it possible for us to control our actions and our desires—what ensures that we are not going to yield to your excesses in life. Moreover, justice is going to refer not to the abstract idea of how each society needs to be done, but it is more about a practice of individuals treating others with fairness and dignity.

One important part of the idea of virtue is that the different virtues all need to be practiced together. You can't have one without the other. You can't be intemperate and courageous at the same time because these go against each other and it just wouldn't work. Although it makes sense for us to say that someone was able to show a lot of courage when they were in battle but then they come home and drink in excess or have a bad temper, the Stoics would not consider this kind of person virtuous. In the view of a Stoic, virtue is an all or nothing ideology. You either are all of the virtues, or you are none of the virtues.

According to a study that was done that compared how virtues are articulated between Taoism, Judaism, Hinduism, Confucianism, Christianity, Buddhism, and Athenian philosophy, it was found that there were six core virtues that were pretty much shared between all of these different world religions. These six ore virtues include:

- Courage: This was considered an emotional strength that would involve the exercise of will in order to accomplish and succeed with goals, even if there is some kind of opposition. This could include things like authenticity, perseverance, and bravery.

- Justice: This would include civic strengths that would underlie a healthy life for the community. You may see things like teamwork, citizenship, leadership, and fairness included in there.

- Humanity: This would include many interpersonal strengths that involve tending and befriending others around you. It would include options like kindness and love.

- Temperance: This would include any strengths that would work to protect against excess. It would include characteristics like self-control, prudence, humility, and forgiveness.

- Wisdom: This would include any cognitive strengths that the individual had that would help them acquire and use knowledge beneficially. Some examples of this would include a perspective so they can provide good counsel to others, judgment, curiosity, and creativity.

- Transcendence: This would be any strength that can forge connections to the larger universe and can provide more meaning for the individual. This may include things like spirituality, hope, and gratitude.

As you can see, four of these six are going to be the exact same as we had talked about with Stoicism. Stoics also accepted the idea of transcendence and humanity, but they didn't count these as virtues. Instead, they were seen more as attitudes towards others and attitudes towards the universe as a whole. These ideas are there—they just aren't necessarily seen in the same way as some of the other religions do. They were good attitudes to have and Stoicism didn't try to discredit them at all. But they viewed them in a different manner than some of the other early religions did. This is amazing though that these virtues are held close by so many different types of religions, ones that are found in all different areas of the world.

Returning back to the virtues, the bigger deal here is not that Stoicism seems to have gotten it right while other religions and traditions didn't. Rather, it is more of the fact that human societies have gone through and developed philosophies to follow in life, and each of them has independently been able to come up with a list that is very similar when they list out their virtues. There can be a whole debate about why this happens and how it could be something deeply rooted in ourselves that make us know those are important virtues.

In modern times, it is hard to have a discussion about the character at all. It has become a big political game. The conservatives often want to bring back the character in schools, the family, and even throughout the country. And then the liberals go through and reject this kind of talk because they think it is just a way to keep white male privilege and patriarchy in place. This is unfortunate because talking about and maintaining character shouldn't be all about the politics at all because it is such an important part of our lives.

Epictetus, as well as other ancients, saw this idea of character as both evolving throughout the development of the individual, as well see it as fundamental to our personal identity. The Stoics believed that no matter what role you play in society, you will still have your character there and that is such an important part of your life.

This is why it is so important to your social life to not only work on improving the character that you hold onto but to be able to assess the character of those around you as well. It doesn't matter what other people may tell you about the character of another. You need to be able to discern it for yourself. Sometimes others will be right with their assessment, but sometimes they will be wrong. So, while you are working with your own character and trying to get it to form and grow in yourself, make sure that you also take the time to watch for and learn about the characters of others.

To be fair, it can be hard to judge the character of someone else if you haven't been able to meet them personally, and when you don't have a history of interacting with them. But give the other person some time before you are quick to judge against them. Just because the first interaction wasn't the best, or just because others are quick to jump in and tell you all that they know about the character of the other person, take your time and don't be too quick to judge someone you have just met.

How will you feel if someone were to quickly judge you? Even the most virtuous of people, the ones who have followed the Stoic philosophy for a long time, will have instances where they stumble and fall. What if you meet with someone new during that fall? Do you want them to judge you wrongly, to think poorly of you because you had a bad time? Or would you rather that they took a few meetings to get to know you, to give you a chance to not have a bad day, before they made their judgments? This is the way that you should treat other people as well for the best results.

To help you develop your character a bit better, you can learn how to practice the four virtues that come with Stoicism. These are so important because they all need to come together in order for you to be seen as virtuous through the eyes of Stoicism. This isn't to be mean, but it does require some work for you to have all four of them in line together. Missing out on one, or only focusing on one at all, can really lead to a lack of character and it is seen as a bad thing by those who follow Stoicism.

If you were looking at some of these different virtues and feel like you come up short, do not fret. Now is the perfect time to start working on them. You can work on all of them at one time, or start with the one that is the most difficult for you. You can then slowly add in each one until you get all of them to work in your life. A Stoic is always going to work to increase their virtues and to do what is right. If you fall a little short, but you are working on them, you are going to be gaining a more virtuous life compared to before.

This is going to take time, and it is going to take a lot of practice. But it is going to bring in a lot of happiness to your life. You will find that the modern world tries to go against you. The modern world is all about instant gratification, about getting things now and doing things that are easy and will bring you more pleasure now.

Those may sound like great ideas right now, but how is that going to work out later in life. How many times have you followed the advice of the modern world, and found out that you were sad, depressed, alone, and a bunch of other negative things? The more you follow what you hear in our modern world of more, the more miserable you will be.

The good news is that by following the virtues of Stoicism to build up your character, you are able to change things around. It is going to be hard sometimes. Sometimes, you may want to give in. But if you follow the virtues that are outlined in Stoicism, and that we outlined a bit earlier in this guidebook, you will find that it is the best path to lead you to true happiness overall.

Chapter 7: Do I Need a Role Model to Be a Stoic?

There are going to be times on your Stoic journey when you run into problems. You may wonder how you are supposed to act in a certain situation. You may wonder whether you are doing the process in the correct manner—or maybe you just have a question that you would like answered, and you are hoping that the wisdom can come from somewhere to help you know how to behave.

When ancient Stoics were wondering what they should do in a situation, they would simply ask the question "What would the sage do?" The Stoics were able to use the idea of a Sage, as a hypothetical ideal in order to help them contemplate and measure themselves against. You can call this Sage a role model or whatever you would like. But it is there as a way to help you figure out what you should do next, and can be a measuring stick any time that you find yourself stuck when practicing Stoicism.

This Stoic Sage is going to be the perfect human being, someone who is very virtuous. This sage is a good person and lives a life that is happy and smoothly flowing. She is everything that all the other Stoics wish they could be because she has no faults and never seems to trip up because of the modern world. This Sage is going to be the best role model when it comes to Stoic philosophy, and this is why so many Stoics will turn to this idea to help them out. Aspiring Stoics will work towards their own perfect wisdom simply by contemplating the Sage. They try to think of how the Sage would react, what the Sage would do. Of course, they have to keep in mind that getting to this perfect ideal is going to be impossible to accomplish. No one, outside of the Sage, can actually get to this level. But it still helps to strive for this level when you are starting your life as a Stoic. Epictetus, a great Stoic teacher, advised many of his students to look at Socrates, someone who was considered the closest to the sage. "Socrates fulfilled himself by attending to nothing except reason in everything that he encountered. And you, although you are not yet a Socrates, should live as someone who at least wants to be a Socrates."

So, if you are looking for a real version of the Sage, someone who you can really look up to and follow their teachings, then Socrates may be the right one. Studying his life, looking through his readings, and building your life up to be similar to his can be a great way to start building Stoicism in your own life.

The What-Would-Batman-Do Study

Now, we are going to take ourselves a little off topic here, but it is going to help us better understand the Stoic Sage and how we can use it to help improve our own lives.

Not many people know about the Stoic Sage. So, we are going to take it a bit further and talk about the Sage as a superhero in today's society. There are some studies that have been done where kids are asked: "What would Batman do?" There have been some interesting tendencies that show up when kids are asked this kind of question. However, these studies are early stage and there is a lot more research that needs to be done. The use of them here is more about fun and the fact that they help us to get an idea of how you can use the Stoic Sage to help yourself.

The first study was meant to help measure the influence of self-distancing on executive function in children who were between three and five years old. In short, this executive function that we are looking at has to do with how well someone can manage their own resources in order to reach their own goal. This study found that an increased distance from self, such as through the perspective of a third person like Batman, ended up improving the executive function in those children.

In a second study, young children were asked to sit down and do a repetitive task for ten minutes, while also having a choice to take breaks and to play a video game. If they were just told to do this, they would easily give up and go and move around to play video games. But when they were given the idea of What Would Batman Do? They had better perseverance to keep doing the repetitive task and they would try to impersonate the behavior that they think Batman would have tried to go with.

In the third study, six to twelve years old where Batman was going to play a big role again. In this method, the children were asked what Batman would eat. After the children asked this question to themselves, they ended up making healthier food choices, such as choosing apple slices instead of French fries in this study. The children who didn't ask what Batman would eat ended up being more likely to pick out the French fries.

As these three studies show, when we hold up our decisions to an ideal, or what we see as an ideal, we are more likely to behave in concordance to that ideal. With the studies above, when the children thought about what heir hero, Batman, would do, they were more likely to make better decisions concerning food and keeping busy and more. And Stoics could use this same idea to help them make the right decisions when they compare any actions they want to undertake with how the Stoic Sage would behave.

It is believed that self-distancing yourself from the situation or the decision by taking on the perspective of a paradigm, which can be the Stoic Sage, Batman like the studies used, or someone else you think is worth following, can help you make better choices in your life. It could be as simple as that to help you become a true Stoic.

How Can the Self-Distancing Help with Decision Making?

When you ask "What would Batman do?" or when you ask what anyone else would do in a situation, you are helping yourself bring in a bit of space between the first impression you have during a situation, and the response that you give. This basically manes that you are bringing in some more awareness to that situation.

The first step to reaching a serious and a lasting change is gaining some awareness. Without having this awareness, change is either incidental or luck based. Think about this. If you do not have an awareness about what is going on, and what is going wrong, in your current life, how are you able to pick the right process, and the right steps, to fix this problem. If you don't realize the why, where, when, how and everything else about your biggest issue and what you want to work on, how are you able to prevent that issue?

As a Stoic, taking the time to contemplate the sage becomes a way of distancing themselves from the situation a little bit. It helps them stop mindlessly following the first impression that they have about a situation. Since Stoics want to be in control of their reactions, and they want to be able to choose the responses that they send out to the world. They don't want to let themselves get caught up in the first impressions they feel, without thinking through the situation logically.

Because of this, you need to be able to test out all the impressions that you have, and then learn how to postpone your response to the situation until a later time. For example, if you don't want to play a game with your kids, or the neighborhood kids, at that time, you could wait a few seconds to determine if that is the right first impression.

You can then ask what the Stoic Sage would do in this situation. From there, you would see that it is best for you to play with your kids for that time.

When you use self-distancing by following a Stoic role model, you refuse to let yourself go with that first, automatic response. You figure out how to check it first and decide if it is the right one you want to go with. Saying "What would Batman do?" or "Impression, wait for me a little" can help bring in some distance to the situation and your reaction. Remember that the impression is just an impression. Just because you have it, doesn't mean the impression is right. As a Stoic, you need to take the time to check it out and check its validity first.

Chose a Role Model for Your Own Life

Now that we have discussed the idea of a Stoic Sage, it is time to pick out the Sage you want to use in your life. You can pick anyone you want. It can be some fictional character that is just a Sage, or you can use Batman or some other hero in your life. You need to keep someone you admire constantly watching you, and constantly checking out everything you do. If you choose to go with Batman, then spend your life acting like Batman is watching you. This can bring more awareness into your daily life, and it ensures that you are going to be more deliberate in the actions you choose.

This is a neat thing about Stoicism; you get the benefit of choosing the person you want to learn from. You don't have to pick just one person at all. You can pick Batman, you can pick God, you can pick a mythical perfect person. You can even choose to work with other Stoics as your Sage. But make sure that you pick out the right Sage that works for you, and then, before making decisions, ask what that Sage would do in that same situation. You may make the same decision after asking this as you would have without asking it. But it helps ensure that you get full control over the situation.

How I Put It All Together

Remember that this isn't about how good you already are. Each person who gets started as a Stoic is going to have different levels of good and bad. But where we start isn't as important. What is important is that you should be all about getting better and improving yourself. To do this, you need to find a role model, and you need to be humble.

So, during this time, find a role model. The good role models are going to be difficult to find in real life. You may have to come up with a fictional character, or someone from the past even, to help you get started. But that seems to be the way of the world. The negative role models can be found when you walk out the door, but the positive role models sometimes have to be created with our own imaginations.

But once you find that positive role model, make sure that they are always ready in your mind. Keep something on you that helps you keep these role models in mind. You can keep a picture of them in your wallet, wear something on your neck or your outfit that will remind you. And then when you end up in some kind of crossroad during your life, you can simply ask what that person would do.

Even if this doesn't give you a full answer and you will have to figure out some of it on your own, this can still be a great thing to add to your day. You will find that just separating yourself out from the situation can help you get the emotions at bay, and will make it easier for you to pick the right decision for your own life in that situation.

So, whenever you get stuck in a situation, and you aren't sure where to go, simply ask yourself

- What would Batman do?
- What would Jesus do?
- What would the Stoic Sage do?
- What would my chosen role model do?

You will quickly find that having someone you admire watching over all of the actions you do can be very beneficial. This brings in a lot more awareness to your current life, and it gives you a way to seek help from those you consider the wisest among us. If nothing else, it at least lets some time pass between any impression you have to a situation and the chosen action you go with.

Chapter 8: How Stoicism Can Help Deal with Mental Illness and Disability

Sometimes, life isn't going to go the way that we would like. We hope that we can be healthy, that we will be able to pay our bills, that we can grow old with a beautiful family, and that everything will go relatively smoothly. However, sometimes, things seem to get in the way. Sometimes, we have to deal with a mental illness—such as autism, anxiety, and depression—or we have to deal with a disability, whether it is severe or just makes regular life difficult to deal with. How would a Stoic deal with these issues?

There are two main aspects of Stoicism that can come into play here. The first one is the insistence that we take a look at the impressions we have or our first reactions to what the world and other people present to us. Then we look at those impressions and realize that in many cases, these impressions and the situations that started them, are not really what they seem.

Let's say that someone came up to us and said something that was mean or hurt our feelings. Whether we perceive the other remark or comment as an insult is going to be completely up to us. It doesn't really matter what the intention of the other person is. Maybe they meant to insult us, and maybe they didn't. But the interpretation of what they said is completely up to us.

There are some different ways that you can look at it. What if the comment is actually true? If it is, then what is the point of getting offended by it? If you don't like that the fact is true, then you need to find ways to improve it rather than getting offended by the things people say. But what if the comment isn't true? Then the other person did it as a childish behavior and they are just talking about things that aren't true. But how does this really injure you? If anything, the other person is the one who is going to lose in this confrontation.

The second Stoic aspect that you can work with here, is the idea of negative visualization, which we talked about a bit before. The basic idea here is that you need to focus regularly on the worst case scenario that can come up with any situation, and then realize that this situation isn't likely to happen and things aren't as bad as they seem. You actually have the inner resources to deal with these. This visualization exercise for the negative may even be able to focus on something as mundane as the irritation, and even anger, that you feel when someone cuts you off on the way to work. It can even be more critical, such as someone you love dying.

At this point, you may wonder why you would want anyone, much less someone who is depressed or dealing with another mental illness, to think about these negative things or the worst scenario. The reason for this is that there is actually an empirical observation that thinking this way actually works. While it sounds a bit counterintuitive, visualizing these negative things can actually decrease our fear of them and can help us prepare mentally to deal with the crisis when, and sometimes if, it ensues.

There is actually a flip side to this kind of negative visualization. While doing it, we start to gain a renewed sense of appreciation for all of the times when that bad thing, or that negative situation, doesn't happen to us. When you imagine getting stuck in traffic and being really late for work, you appreciate a leisurely drive where there are hardly any roadblocks at all. When we think about losing the ones that we love, we learn how to value our time with them more and have a better time when we meet up with them.

Now, there are a lot of different ways that you can approach mental illness in your life and even disability. But the Stoic principles can come into play here as well. Some people misunderstand how Stoicism works, and they assume that they aren't going to be able to get any help for these issues through the Stoic philosophy. They think that Stoicism is all about being unemotional and unattached to other things. But this isn't true. Since Stoicism is more about helping an individual to be more in control of their emotions, and to accept the things that they can't control, and this can help out so many people who are dealing with issues like depression and anxiety and more.

How Stoicism Can Help with Depression and Anxiety

The first topic we are going to discuss here is how Stoicism is able to help with various mental illnesses. The two most common of these that people deal with include depression and anxiety. Both of these disorders can be tough for the individual to deal with. Sometimes they go together, and other times they will be two separate things that can make life difficult for the individual. The good news is that Stoicism can help with both of these issues.

First, we can look at depression. With depression, the symptoms can take a lot of different forms, and each person who is dealing with it will experience it in a different way. Some sufferers may seem sad, and others don't. Some individuals with this may have complaints of not being able to get up and move, or feeling like they are unmotivated about anything. They may find that doing simple tasks, such as getting dressed or eating at mealtime, can become really big obstacles in their daily life. In some cases, family and friends may even notice that there are these changes to, and they want to help, but they are not sure what to do.

When these things happen, you may be able to use Stoicism to make a difference. Depression can be caused by a lot of different things, but the symptoms can often make little situations in life, seem like really big deals. This is back to the idea of learning what you can control, and what you can't.

With depression, you may find that you feel overwhelmed and like things are too difficult to handle. You may not be able to control this, but you can change how you react to it. For example, instead of just letting that overwhelming sense come over you, you can decide to take sand and chase it off. Now, with depression, this can be easier said than done in many cases. But starting out with something simple, such as a smile when you feel overwhelmed, can change your perception. When those feelings come over, you can learn to take deep breaths, get yourself into a new situation that can make you happier, or even choose to say something like "I choose to be happy today."

This does take some time. Depression can be a serious issue and one that many people struggle with for a long time. And Stoicism isn't there to just tell you to get over it and move on. But it can be there to help you manage your depression a bit better than you might be doing now. With some change in perception, and some help from your doctor and others you trust, you can use Stoicism and other methods to help you deal effectively with your depression.

Now we can move on to the idea of anxiety. Anxiety is going to be a bit different. Many people will feel anxious about small little things in their lives, but those who feel the mental illness of anxiety will often get nervous and upset in such a way that they have trouble functioning. They worry about a situation and what will happen. This can cause them to freeze up and get so anxious and overwhelmed in that situation, that they are not able to function in a normal manner.

Many times this anxiety gets so bad that the sufferer will decide to avoid situations that trigger the anxiety. Often this means big changes to their lives. They may walk a certain way home. They may avoid social situations. Some will only take certain jobs because they worry about anxiety. Anxiety can easily become a problem when it starts to take over your life and makes it difficult for you to even do the things that you enjoy.

The biggest issue that can come with anxiety is a desire to control things, and then having issues when you find that you can't control these things. People with anxiety find that they do the best when they can stay home, or in situations where they are in full control. When they leave that area of control, the panic and anxiety attacks begin to take over.

When you use the ideas of Stoicism in order to let go of this idea that you need to control everything, you may find that your anxiety can improve. There are going to be situations in your life that you can't control. Coming to this understanding can make life easier to handle. You can let go of that and instead focus on the things that you can control. Negative visualization can come into play here as well. When you prepare for the worst case scenario, and you focus on the things that you can control, such as the way you react to situations, and you learn how to let go of the things that you can't control, you will find that those panic attacks and those anxiety attacks will slowly start to go away.

How Stoicism Can Help with Disabilities

There are many different types of disabilities. Some are temporary and may leave us tied up and slowed down for just a small moment in time. Others are more permanent. Some may only affect us a bit, and some may make life very difficult indeed and can make life as a whole difficult to work with. No one wishes to have a disability, but many people don't take the time to appreciate the fact that they are healthy and able to do things on their own.

When you have a disability, it is easy to get upset with the world. You are mad that you have lost the ability to do things. You may be upset about how hard life can be. You may even be upset and angry at the way that people look and react around you now. Many people who are dealing with disabilities find that they sink into depression and other mental illnesses as well, especially when they find that they are left behind or they worry about what others think of them, and they decide to isolate themselves from others.

In this situation, there are two different parts; the things that you can control, and the things that you can't. To start, you can't control that you have this disability. Something happened and now you have this disability. It isn't a lot of fun, but there is nothing that you can do about it. If the disability will get better over time, you can certainly work to make it better, but since most disabilities are more permanent, it is time to realize that the situation happened and there is nothing that you can do to change it.

This isn't meant to be harsh or cruel to someone who has suffered a disability. But when you change your perception of the situation, you will find that you can get through it much better. Rather than lamenting on how bad the situation is and feeling bad about it, you can realize that the situation happened, you didn't have any control over it, and now it is time to concentrate less on that, and more on the things that you can actually control.

No matter how bad the situation is, there are some things that you can control about your disability. To start, you can control your attitude and your thoughts about the disability. Instead of being upset that something bad happened to you—instead, focus on the attitude that you would like to present to the world. Consider looking at the bright side of things. Think about how you are still alive, think about the things that you are able to still do, and think about the people you still get to see.

A change of attitude can make a big difference in how well you can handle this new situation or a situation you were born with. You will be more positive. You will find new ways to make life easier for yourself. You will take the time to get out of the home and see people, which can help improve your mood even more than before.

Stoicism can help you work on this. Remember that there is a lot in Stoicism about focusing on the things that you can change and control, and letting go of the things that you have no control over. This can be hard when you see the things that other people can do, or the things that other people have, but you will find that doing this can improve your life and make you so much happier in every aspect of your life, no matter what situation is going on around you. Stoicism can help out so many different aspects of your life. It may seem like a philosophy that only works for individuals who are happy and have life easy, but in reality, it can work for anyone who is looking to improve their lives, who want to learn how to be happier, and who want to see an improvement. Those who feel that they are down on their luck, or like life is out of control are the ones who can profit the most from Stoicism, as we have seen from this chapter. Everyone can gain some insight and some benefits from working with Stoicism, they just need to learn how to implement it in their own lives.

Part 3: How to React to Things That Happen Around Us

Chapter 9: Stoics Views on Suicide and Death

Now, it is time to take a look at death and what it means to many modern Stoics. The idea of death is something that really terrifies many people. Even those who believe in a God or another deity find that the idea of death can paralyze them, terrify them, and keep them up at night sometimes. Death is something that is going to come for us all at some point. None of us know when it is going to come, though, and we don't know for sure what is going to follow afterward—and this can be scary.

Right now, we know what we have in our current lives. We know we have our homes, we know what to expect, and we know that it is comforting. Not knowing what is going to happen after we die can torture the minds of individuals all throughout history. This is a great mystery, something that is unknown and pretty scary for most people, and it can be a big fear as well.

With all this worry and fear about death through the ages, you will find that Stoic philosophy is actually set up to help you know more about how to live a good life, and how we are supposed to view death. Central to the philosophy of Stoicism are three disciplines including will, action, and perception. Just as these three things are useful in the manner we live now, these three can also give us a comprehensive approach to death under the Stoic philosophy as well.

Perception

The first thing that we are going to take a look at is perception. Perception is going to be our field of vision. It is the way that we as an individual sees things and it's our field of thought. And what we think and what we see are going to shape the things that we do. Perception is one of the defining principles behind the Stoic thought on cognition. To understand perception, it is important for us to understand this kind of theory because it is a universal order of Stoic philosophy.

Humans have been given the ability to think things through, something that no other animal on earth can do. We have the capacity to use our perception in order to see an event as either evil or good, based just on our interpretation after an initial impression. The Stoics are going to call this the faculty of reason, and with this, they said that there isn't such a thing as evil or good; these are just a product of each individual personal judgment.

In the translation of Meditations that was done by Gregory Hays, this idea is explained in three parts. To put it simply, something happens, it is going to produce some kind of expression in our minds, and then we are going to turn that into our own perception of the situation. This perception is going to include how we see that thing or situation, how we interpret that meaning, and more. In a way, we always have the power of choice.

The Stoics spent a lot of time and energy thinking about and trying to master their perception because they knew how important perception was to shaping behavior. If our perceptions are clouded, colored with nonsense, or if they have been changed by other things in our environment, it is possible for things like unhappiness, trepidation, lack of confidence, anxiety, and fear are able to get into it. You can think of the process of these perceptions forming in a way similar to how you form habits. Habits are going to start due to hearing, practicing, and then saying things, in the same way, one day after another. Perceptions are going to be similar in that they will become ingrained through repeated thought and practice over time.

Because of this, perceptions have the ability to be a powerful source of strength and resolve, or you can use them the wrong way and they become a big source of horror and weakness. The good news here is that you are the one who is in control with this situation. You get to make the choice on how you will perceive any situation, including death, and you can make that perception be anything that you would like.

As this topic relates back to death, the disciplining of your perception can become your ally when it comes to silencing and turning off the terror that you feel about death. By learning how to take control of your perceptions and wielding them in the proper way, you can stop that fear, even towards death. Often we fear death because we have trained ourselves to feel this way. We have the impression that when life ends, that endless void needs to be devastating and tragic.

But when we learn how to change our perceptions of death, it doesn't feel as scary as before. But how can we change our views on death and look at it differently? You can start by thinking about death as something better. Rather than seeing it as an endless void that is scary, you can consider thinking about it as a place where you get to come to rest, a place where you get to meet up with your old friends and family members. You can choose any method that you would like to think about death, but a simple change in perception can really help improve how you handle it overall.

Action

Perception is all about learning how to reinterpret death. However, action is going to be more about what we decide to do about that perception to death. What are we going to do about this fear? Are you letting that fear bother and torment you? Are you trying to just push it out of your mind until it rears its head again? Remember that with this one it is all about conquering your fears and being the one who is in control.

If you become passive to death, it can become harrowing and it is going to become stronger over time. Death can do well as both a polarizing and a paralyzing subject. We don't really want to talk about it, think about it, or even imagine it happening to us. But go back to the idea of negative visualization that we have brought up in this guidebook and let that be your guide. There are times when you may want to talk about, think about, and even imagine death and what it would be like. This helps get the hold of death off us and can really make it seem less scary overall.

Ancient Stoics have learned to make it part of their routine to always have the idea of death in mind. This isn't meant to be a really morbid practice. In fact, it was meant to be the opposite. The torture that comes from the idea of death is often from the fact that we hold onto death as something scary. We feel that there is too much uncertainty that comes from death, and this makes all of us scared. We know that it is going to happen, but we don't know when it will happen, how it will happen, or what will occur when it does happen.

Now, many people feel that death is something that they should push back. They worry that talking about it and worrying about it is just going to make it seem more real, and they are worried about it. But when you take the time to think about death and what it really means, and you think about the worst case scenario that can come with death, you can then start to see that things aren't that bad, and you can then focus more on enjoying life.

This can sometimes seem like a hard thing. We are not happy thinking and talking about the unknown. We just want to push it all back and never think about it at all. But this just makes the thought of death scarier than before. When you do think about it and talk about it, then the situation isn't so bad. Taking action to do this and to chase the fear away can make a big difference in how you handle death while you are alive.

Will

And the third discipline that is devoted to death and life in Stoicism is known as will. The Stoics were able to categorize all things into two buckets. One bucket known as internals and the other was externals. The internals are simply the things that we are actually able to have some control over. This would be the things like action and perception that we talked about before. These are both going to be choices that we have control over.

However, the idea of the externals is going to be the opposite. These externals are going to be the things that we don't really have any control over. And the will is going to be the attitude that we bring to the table when things occur that aren't in our control.

No matter how hard you try, there are just some things in life that you aren't able to control. People will act in a certain way, there will be extra work that you have to get done, the kids get grumpy, someone gets in an accident on your way to work and you end up late and more. Our will is the way that we end up handling and reacting to any situation that is not really in our own control.

The discipline that comes with will, may at first glance seem like it goes against the perception and action topics that we talked about before. But in reality, these are going to align together nicely. We are powerless over all of the external events that occur in our lives, except for the power we hold to determine what these all mean and how we are going to respond to them.

The will that we are talking about here is going to hold all of this power, as long as it is disciplined in cultivating indifference to the things that we are not able to control, to influence all of our perceptions and then decide how we are going to respond. This kind of will can be useful because it does provide you with another option when it comes to overcoming how fearful you are over the idea of death and dying.

You will notice that there are some similarities with will and perception and how it is used to change how we look at death—the will is going to take this a bit further. The will is not just about changing the way that you look at death, but it also helps you gain acceptance that death is what nature, what the universe, had intended for us in the end. It is something that is going to happen to everyone—and being able to accept that, without all the worry, can lead to a lot more happiness in the long run.

According to Cicero and Seneca, death is not something to be feared because it isn't seen as something that is happy or unhappy. If death happens to turn out to be a black hole with nothing in it, then this means that in the end, we have no pain and no consciousness. We will have peace in the end if this happens, and who is scared or fearful about peace?

On the other hand, maybe there is eternal life, just like all the religions and spiritual thoughts have promised for years. If this eternal life does wait for us, then this is a great thing. Why would we fear death and this eternal life when it is nothing but good for us in the afterlife?

The Stoic view on death is quite a bit different than what most people may be used to when talking about these topics. Many people have taught themselves to be scared about death. Even if they are following one of the major religions and have a good idea on what the afterlife can be like, many are still scared that things won't be how they imagined when they die. They may be worried about not coming back, about having an eternal void they have to deal with, and other things about death simply because it is something that is unknown and something that they can't control.

But with the ideas that come with Stoicism, death is neither good or bad. It is something that is going to happen at some point. Accepting this can really make a difference. Using perception, action, and will about death can make a big difference as well. It helps you see death as a natural part of our lives, a continuation, rather than being scared and upset about it and wasting all those precious years on earth thinking about it. Death is not something to be scared of or something to fret and worry about. Death is a natural part of our lives, and it can lead us to more happiness in life when we learn how to keep the fear and uncertainty out of the mix.

Chapter 10: How to Deal with Negative Emotions

One of the biggest misconceptions that we will see concerning Stoicism is that it is seen as a philosophy that is based on having no emotions. It is important to realize that Stoics *do* have emotions—they just know how to use those emotions more to their benefit compared to other people. Stoics know how to not let their emotions define them or guide them. It's not really that the emotions aren't a factor or that the person is able to live their life without ever feeling and emotion—but the Stoic realizes that they do still have control, regardless of what emotion is present, and they realize that emotions should never be the only component in their lives.

Another thing to consider is the idea of passion. Many people in our modern world say they have a passion for something. But when it comes to the Stoics, passion is going to be more of a taboo subject because they see passion as an emotion with very little reasoning behind it. It is possible to have a ton of passion for something—but how realistic are these feelings in your life?

Stoics are known for their rationality, and they realize that their emotions are often the culprit as to why others aren't able to use reason when making decisions. In a sense, the way that Stoics are able to handle their emotions is like a type of meditation. They take the time to analyze the situation at hand, a face value, weigh out how beneficial the emotional reactions are, and then decide how they want to respond. They may find in most cases that the reaction isn't going to serve much purpose when it is compared to the intended outcome.

There is no doubt that some of the negative emotions we are faced with on a regular basis are a type of warning system during some of the situations in our lives. This becomes a problem though when the negative emotions start to go out of control and keep taking over long past what the warning system requires. There really is no reason for us to be constantly reviewing your negative thoughts, or letting yourself become engulfed by them. But this is what happens to most people.

We don't really need our emotions to be a warning system in our modern world. There are plenty of other warning systems found in our society. By looking through the media, and analyzing things on a daily basis, we don't need to become the negative emotions that we feel. Being apprehensive and paranoid may have been a great survival instinct to early man when the world was more hostile. But now, we don't need to feel these things and keeping them around is harming our physical wellbeing and driving us to make poor decisions.

Stoics are able to pride themselves on living in a state that is more tranquil, one that has very little, and sometimes no negative emotional impact, something that everyone else who is starting out can strive for. But even the Stoics aren't perfect in this regard. There are still times when they will struggle and run into difficulties. But the important part is to still work at it until you are able to get it right.

The most important thing to remember about emotions is that when they gain control, you are going to lose out on your reasoning capabilities. Emotions do not understand the reason, and this can lead you to react in ways that you may not be proud of if you let the emotions out. Stoics value reasoning overall, so learning how to reign in and control those emotions can be very important if you want to become a Stoic.

Of course, this doesn't mean that negative emotions can't be useful in some cases with a Stoic. For example, we have already talked about the use of negative visualization as a stoic exercise. When someone is able to create the worst case scenario, view it over, analyze it a bit, and more, this can help take away some of the power that the situation holds. When you already know the worst that can happen and embrace that is the most probable cause, then you will find that the situation doesn't bother you as much any longer. And when the situation turns out better than you had anticipated, this can be great news that makes you happier overall.

Another angle of using this negative visualization and the emotions that are associated with it is how you would present your ideas, and your goals, consciously. If you had the ability to wake up each day and tell yourself that you are going to play in the NBA, but in reality, you are horrible at playing basketball—you are basically setting yourself up for failure. Now, this may seem pretty obvious, but telling yourself what will happen is a great way to encounter those negative emotions if you don't meet the goal.

With the example above, you are basically putting yourself inside a box, rather than being realistic about the idea that the goal may not happen. And since you are just dreaming big and not using negative visualization, you are going to run into a wall and feel a lot of negative emotions when the ending isn't the way that you want it.

A Stoic's mindset is not just going to focus on the goal, but they will also focus on the path that gets them there. This helps them get to their end, to the end of the path, while feeling indifferent about it. Sure, you want to reach your goals in life—that is why we are coming up with a path to get there. But in reality, all we can do is try to achieve the goal, but we can't make the assumption that it will happen for us. If you aren't a good basketball player, it doesn't matter how much you wish or hope to be on the NBA, you will never get there.

When a Stoic is able to think in this manner, they are effectively creating an insurance policy that has realistic expectations of failure. This may sound like a bad thing, but it can actually work to make life better. You know ahead of time that things may not work out, and that is fine. You focus on reaching your goal, but you keep the path open in case things don't work out the way that you want all the time.

At this point, you may be wondering why you should work so hard towards a goal if the Stoic ideology wants you to disregard the end goal. Remember that this process is not that the Stoic isn't thinking about the end goal. It's more about the fact that the real goal is to do what he is able to do right now and then become indifferent to the outcome, no matter what it may be.

This doesn't mean that the Stoic is passive and that they go into a new set of goals not hoping for a positive outcome. It is more about the Stoic being in enough emotional control where they are able to handle whatever is going to come their way in the future. The Stoic will work on the things they can control when it comes to this goal, but then they realize that there may be things outside their control that can make the end result different than planned.

For a non-Stoic, getting an end result that isn't positive, or a result that isn't what they planned, could be disastrous. They will get upset and mad, and their emotions may start to take over. They may scream at others, lament that life isn't being fair to them, go home and sulk, and even say and do things to the ones they love that they regret later on. This is a sign that the emotions have started to take over, and is the opposite of what a good Stoic would like to see.

Stoics adopt this different manner of thinking because they know it allows them to be the ones in control over their own emotions. They refuse to let the emotions take control, so they start out a new path, or a new expectation, assuming that there may be things that they can't control, and there is a chance that the result isn't going to turn out the way they want it to. Of course, the Stoic wants to have a positive outcome for their work or for the situation, but a true Stoic knows that this isn't going to happen all the time, so they mentally prepare themselves in case it doesn't.

Even if you are not planning on becoming a true Stoic, there is still so much you can learn from this outlook on situations and events that happen to you. Think of it this way, if you spend your time so fixated on controlling things and on the end game, think about all of the experiences you are going to miss on the journey. This can make the completion either less attainable or less desirable than it was before.

A Stoic is going to work towards making every experience a good one, no matter the situation they are in. They are going to make sure that their approach is holistic, not stuck on any one part, and the Stoic will learn how to be indifferent, or happy with, any outcome that occurs. This can be difficult depending on the type of personality that you have. But when you take the time to practice it, you will find that it produces an outcome that is more favorable.

Controlling your emotions, especially the negative emotions, is the cornerstone of living a life that is considered Stoic. To gain true happiness in your life, it is important to learn how to be the one in control—and changing the way that you perceive each situation is sometimes the best way to ensure that you are going to be able to control your emotions. In many cases, this part is going to be the most difficult part to work on when it comes to Stoicism. But with some dedication, and with some 'picking yourself back up if you fall', you will be able to make this work for you.

Chapter 11: Friendship and Love in a Stoic Life

And now, before we end out this section, it is time to take a look at love and friendship and how the Stoics viewed these interactions. While many people see the Stoics as emotionless and passionless, this doesn't mean that they thought that love was a negative emotion that they had to kick out of their lives. In fact, both Seneca and Marcus Aurelius write lovingly about their wives many times. Seneca, who ended up losing his only child, captures the love of parenting so beautifully in his writing, that it is easy to see how much love and care he had for his family.

In addition, Cato, known as a towering Roman Stoic, clearly had a lot of affection for his daughter as can be seen in his writings. And Epictetus would argue on several occasions that only the lover of rationality and wisdom can truly understand and appreciate love the way that it was meant to be.

The point of this is that the Stoics did love, and they did so unashamedly and deeply. However, they would often do it in their own unique way, in a way that was different from other schools of thought at the time, especially the Romantic. While the Romantic only understood love in its unrequited form, the Stoic would approach emotions, such as love, from a more philosophical outlook. For a Stoic, it was fine to love, but it was important to not let yourself be driven to madness with any love.

For example, how many times has a young man been obsessed with love for a young woman, and then gone on to do a lot of irrational and embarrassing things? If you go after love and let it control you, then you are going to be using love in the wrong manner. This doesn't mean that you should forget about love and never experience love. You just need to make sure that you don't let love take control over everything, or it could end up being your ruin and it could take away your freedom.

There are a lot of writings about love when it comes to the ancient Stoic philosophers. For example, Epictetus describes how unhappy a person will be when they become a slave, even to the one they love. Arius Didymus refers often to an unruly and lustful type of love, one that takes away the reasoning that we should have.

Seneca spends some time talking about the blinding grief that someone often feels when they lose someone they really love, either by death or by distance. But then Seneca would always return to love as the best method to use to move away from the grief, rather than becoming overwhelmed by the grief that you are feeling.

So, while it is true that the Stoics did love, they also had some worries that too much love, or love used in the wrong way, could lead to odds with their overall philosophy. Stoic happiness is a life that is lived free from fear, grief, pain and desire, and one without passion. Because of this reason, when a Stoic person thinks about love, it is often going to be put in relation to their higher principles, extolling virtue and comparing his love of pleasure, wealth, glory, and more.

Many Stoics also practiced ways to balance out that love so that it didn't take over their lives too much. For example, one exercise that you could do in concerns to love is talking through it and exploring your feelings so that you do not give in to excess too much.

This doesn't mean that you can't love the people in your lives. As we have mentioned, there are a lot of Stoics who have written about the people they loved in their lives. Having love in your life, and friendships can make a big difference when it comes to how happy your life is going to be. Don't go into the idea of Stoicism thinking that you should live life with no love or friendship at all, and don't try to live a life like this.

The difference though is that you need to think about love in a rational way. Think about someone you know who fell madly in love one time. The love didn't make much sense. It seemed to move quickly and the person you knew wasn't acting like themselves, maybe getting angry when others misspoke about their chosen love. They may have stopped doing other things that they loved just to hang out with this one person. Perhaps they seemed like they were on a high, and the only thing they could think or talk about was that person.

Even though everyone else could see it, the friend missed out on warning signs that the other person wasn't right for them. Hey kept with the relationship, perhaps moving too quickly and getting married without really knowing the other person, assuming that love was enough to get them through. They may have moved to a new city, gotten a new job, and changed up their lifestyle all because the person they loved asked them to.

Now, this doesn't mean that the other person didn't love your friend, and it doesn't mean that they had any evil intentions during this process either. They may have acted just as irrationally during that time and may have fallen trap to the emotions taking control as well. Either way, both of these people are now in a relationship of love, following along where their emotions take them, rather than using any reasoning in the process.

People who fall in love at first sight will often let their emotions get the best of them. They sometimes even use this as an excuse for the way they behave or the way that they treat others. But this is completely against the beliefs that most Stoics have and can be a dangerous way to live your life.

Stoics take a slightly different method of finding love and being with someone. They may have times when they fall madly in love with someone they just met. But instead of just jumping right in and following their own emotions, they choose to take a different course instead. When they meet this person, they stop and think it through, and they take things slowly. Rather than just jumping in and moving in with the other person right away, they will take their time to get to know the other person.

They may take the other person on a few dates and get to know them. They will figure out whether the two of them are compatible. When they feel some intense emotions, they will take the time to think through their emotions, to talk it out, before jumping in and acting rash. They know that it is fine to be in love and to love someone else, but they also realize that they still need to think rationally about things, and not let the emotion of love take over.

While the Stoics are not going to compromise with their philosophic principles, they can still allow themselves to use a wide range of responses, as long as they moderate those responses and base them on correct understanding and judgment. Remember that the deposition of a Stoic is to always be active and in control of the situation, always vigilant and never passive in these cases.

The idea of love for a Stoic is one that is moderated by a sense of loss in the future, by the potential for betrayal, from the chance that our feelings towards that person could also change over time. After accepting these conditions, the irrational of these powerful feelings of love become a bit more rational, and the life of a Stoic is more manageable.

As someone who loves virtue, the Stoic is able to recognize when others have virtue as well. And since this kind of disposition is the foundation for the happiness of a Stoic, unrequited love is just seen as absurd to the Stoic. Due to the active disposition, the Stoic lover is going to spend their time worrying more about giving love to other people, rather than receiving it. They do enjoy receiving love from other people, but they follow the idea that it is better to give than to receive when it comes to love. Once they find someone worthy of their love, and they know that this love will allow them to still pursue what is important to them and allow them to think rationally, then the Stoic is more than happy to share their love with that person.

A Stoic is attuned to what is known as the whole, the whole of the world, the whole universe, the whole of mankind. And in a sense, the Stoic is loved for it. Stoics have love not only for family and friends but also for other people all throughout the world. Remember that we had talked about how Stoics felt that you should focus on mankind, rather than just your own country or your own tribe. The idea of love can fit in with this as well.

Equipped with this thought, the Stoic is able to return to the battlefield that is known as love. The Stoic knows that love can easily cause you to lose control over things, and it can make it difficult to think in a rational way. But the Stoic is able to approach the idea of love like a general, coming in with a strategic plan and a cool head. Along with the other precepts that come with the Stoics, he is going to carry the antidotes that come with the excess of the Romantics. He is ready to love others in his life, but he won't let himself fall in love completely and lose his reason. And if he does end up falling, he has the tools to pick himself back up again afterward.

As a Stoic, you are welcome to love. Love your friends. Love your spouse or the one you are with. Love your children. Most of all, love anyone else who is important in your life—and when you love them, make sure to do it deliberately and deeply. The Stoic philosophy is not against love and everything that comes with it. Instead of just jumping into this and making rash decisions without reason, take a clear-headed approach. Instead of falling in love, choose to be in love with the other person. This can lead to a deeper connection than you can imagine, allows both you and the other person to keep your own unique personalities without giving anything up, and can lead to a deeper love with that person.

Part 4: Spiritual Exercises to Become a Stoic

Chapter 12: The Best Exercises to Create a Stoic in You

Now that we have spent some time talking about Stoicism and all of the great ways that it can help improve your life, it is time to implement some Stoic exercises into your life. These exercises are going to help you get the most out of the philosophy when you want to add it into your own life. Some of the best exercises to work with include the following.

Practice Misfortune

While all of us want to have all the good in our lives and be able to avoid the bad, it is important to really practice misfortune when we get the chance. This may sound bad, but it helps train us to see that things really aren't as bad as we thought. When we worry about losing food, losing our homes, losing our jobs, we become worried and anxious about these things.

But when you practice misfortune and let it come into your life, you learn that it isn't as bad as you thought. If you were worried about not having a job, you learn how to think in this way. You learn that there are other jobs, that you do have enough in savings to handle a job loss, and you learn that you can handle whatever life throws at you. When you are worried about not getting enough to eat, and you practice sometimes without eating, you find that missing a few meals isn't that big a deal.

Practicing misfortune is the best way to ensure that you are prepared no matter how life turns out. Some of the situations that occur to you in life are beyond your control. But others, like how you react to those situations, are completely within your control. When you practice misfortune, you learn that it isn't that bad, and you can then react to what reaction you send out to the world.

Train Your Perception to See Things Differently

"Choose not to be harmed, and you won't feel harmed. Don't feel harmed, and you haven't been". The Stoics had a great exercise that they called Turning the Obstacle Upside Down. What this is going to mean is that the individual should make it impossible to not practice philosophy in their daily life. Because if you are able to turn any problem upside down, all of the bad in your life will become good. There isn't any good or bad when it comes to practicing Stoicism. There is only the perception of things, and we assign meaning to them as either good or bad. You can choose to tie your perceptions to the situation in any manner that you choose. But learning that everything can be good or bad, and it is how we perceive them, and how we learn to use them, that will be the ultimate determinant in the end.

Remember That Everything Is Ephemeral

Many times we will talk about passions in this guidebook. Passions aren't used in the way that we often see in our modern language. When a Stoic is overcoming their passions, they are referring to irrational, unhealthy, and excessive desires and emotions. Anger is a good example of one of these passions. What is important to remember is that the Stoic is trying to replace these negative emotions with better things, like joy and happiness.

To return back to the point of this exercise, you need to remember how small you are. Remember the fact that achievements are small, and you are just going to hold onto them for an instant—and no longer. If everything is ephemeral like this, then what does it all matter? The only thing that matters is *right now*. Being a good person and learning how to do what is right at the moment is what's important.

Try to See Things from Above

Another thing that you can practice is an exercise that is known as taking the view from above. It invites you to step back from the situation, zoom out, and see your own life from a vantage point that is not your own. This helps you find a new perspective and reminds you of how small you, and that situation, are. This can help us to understand that each situation isn't necessarily a big deal, and maybe we don't need to overreact to each thing that happens to us. Seeing how small we are when it comes to the grand scheme of things is actually just a part of this exercise. The next part that the Stoics will use is known as *sympatheia*, or a mutual interdependence with the whole of humanity. This step is all about taking a step back from the situation, especially when it seems to be going negatively, and reminding yourself that it isn't that big of a deal in the grand scheme of things.

Think About Your Own Mortality

Another part that comes with Stoicism is the idea of reflecting on mortality. According to Meditations done by Marcus Aurelius, "You could leave life right now. Let that determine what you do and say and think." This was meant to be a personal reminder for individuals to live a life of virtue at this time, rather than waiting to do it later.

Meditating on your own mortality is only going to be depressing if you think about it in the wrong way. The Stoics find that this thought humbling and invigorating. They like the idea that they are able to choose to live the best life now because you never know when things are going to end for you. You can choose to live a life of virtue, you can choose to enjoy life, and you can make it your best life right now. While other people are brought down and sad about death, the Stoic learns how to appreciate life when talking about their own mortality.

Think About Whether the Situation Is in Your Control

The biggest part of the Stoic philosophy is that the individual who practices it needs to be able to differentiate between the things they have the power to change, and the things that they don't. Too many times we base our lives and our emotions on things that we really have no control over. But is it really worth having this kind of attitude about things that we can't really do anything about?

For example, your flight might get delayed due to the weather. It doesn't matter how much you yell at the airline representative, but the storm is there and the plane is not going to move. Wishing that you were born taller or shorter, or wishing that you were born in a different country, are all things that we can't control. And the time you spend hurting yourself about these uncontrollable things is time wasted.

Each day, you need to consider what you can control and what you are not able to control. This alone can really help increase the amount of happiness that you experience in your life. You learn to handle the things that are within your control, and you let go of the things that you can't do much about.

Spend Some Time Journaling

Journaling can be a great exercise when it comes to learning how to be a Stoic. The art of journaling in Stoicism is more than just doing a simple diary. This practice is more of a philosophy. This can help you prepare for the day ahead, reflect on the day that passed, and remind yourself of all the wisdom that you learned throughout the day.

You can choose the method that you want to use to get started with journaling. Some people like to journal in the morning because it helps them reflect on what they would like to have happened during the day, and it is a great way to prepare for what is going to happen. Or, you can do it at the end of the day to help you reflect on the lessons that were learned during that day and to make sure that you remember them.

Practice Negative Visualization

Another Stoic exercise that you can work on is the pre-meditation of evils. This is an exercise where the individual is going to imagine all the things that they could lose or all the things that could go wrong. The reason that they do this is that the visualization can help prepare someone for the inevitable setbacks that may occur in life. There are going to be times when we don't get what we want, even if we worked hard to get there. Not everything is going to be fair or work out the way that we want. Preparing our minds for this can be a great way to build up our strength and our resilience.

For example, Seneca would start out by reviewing or rehearsing his plans to do something—like take a trip. Then, in his head, or even journaling it out like our other suggestion, he would go over all of the things that could go wrong or something that could prevent him from going on the trip.

There is nothing that will happen to the wisest of men against their expectations. If you plan for the worst, then nothing is going to surprise or upset you when things don't go well. It is unlikely that things will end up as the worst—which means that you are prepared ahead of time—and you *will* have a better time than predicted.

Conclusion

Thank you for making it through to the end of *Stoicism*, let's hope it was informative and able to provide you with all of the tools you need to achieve your goals—whatever they may be.

The next step is to take some time to implement a little bit of Stoicism into your own life. As we saw in this book, there are so many different aspects that can come with the idea of Stoicism. Many people get the wrong impression when it comes to Stoicism. They feel that these kinds of people have no emotions, that they don't really care about those around them, and that they don't have any of their own emotions. However, as we discussed, Stoics have plenty of emotions. They are humans just like the rest of us, and those emotions come and go just like they do with everyone else—but the difference is that a Stoic has learned how to control those emotions. Rather than letting those emotions get out of hand and take over, the Stoic gets the benefit of being able to feel an emotion, step back from it, and determine whether that emotion needs to be displayed at that moment or not.

That is just one part of being a Stoic, though. There is so much that comes with this kind of personality and this kind of person. As we discussed throughout this guidebook, Stoicism not only helps you learn how to control your emotions, but it can help you reduce stress, anger, frustration, and other negative emotions because it teaches you how to let go of the things that are not in your control. No matter how much we may wish it, life is going to happen, and we just can't control everything. Understanding this—and allowing it to happen in our lives—is a way to gain happiness through Stoicism.

Inside this book, we also took some time to discuss more about Stoicism, the different virtues that come with Stoicism, how it compares to some other religions that are in the world and if it would match up with them or work on its own, how to use Stoicism to build up stronger relationships with others around you, and so much more.

The best thing about Stoicism is that it isn't tied to one religion or one group of people. It is a philosophy that anyone can implement in their lives. It is all about being a virtuous person and about finding your true happiness—and that is something that everyone in the world can benefit from.

While the ideas from Stoicism may have come from the ancient world, there are still many lessons that we can learn and come to understand in our modern lives. In fact, we may find that we need Stoicism and its philosophies more now than they were needed in the past. When you are ready to learn more about Stoicism and how to implement this school of thought in your life, make sure to check out this guidebook to help you get started.

Finally, if you found this book useful in any way, a review on Amazon is always appreciated!

RETAIL AUDIO SAMPLE

Have you been feeling like something is missing? Do you often feel like your emotions get the best of you and that you do and say things that you don't really mean? Do you run into trouble with relationships and others at home, at work, in business or whatever because you feel like you need to control the situation—but the situation tends to do whatever it wants instead?

This is the way many of us live our modern lives. We feel unhappy and alone—and oftentimes, we let our emotions determine what is going to happen next.

However, this is a miserable way to live life. There will always be things in our lives that we wish we could control but can't—and getting upset and letting negative emotions take over can lead us to have a reaction that doesn't fit with the situation.

This is where the idea of Stoicism can come into play. Instead of letting something else be in control, we learn how to make ourselves the ones leading our lives. Being able to do this is at the core of Stoicism and how it can benefit everyone.

While we can't control all of the situations and things that happen in our lives, we can have control over the way that we react and behave with these situations.

This audiobook is going to give you a comprehensive overview of all the powerful teachings, principles and practical spiritual exercises contextualized in our modern life that have been adopted by some of the most successful philosophers in history.

This audiobook will take some time to discuss Stoicism and the various parts that come with its teachings. There is so much to learn and love about Stoicism—even in our modern world. Some of the topics that we will discuss concerning Stoicism and how it can help us improve our lives include:

- What Stoicism is all about;
- How to understand when some things are in our power and some are not;
- How to live according to nature—rather than against it;
- The virtues and character of a true Stoic
- Why material possessions aren't going to lead to happiness;
- How to deal with anxiety, depression and negative emotions
- Practical ways to become a better friend and a perfect partner
- The importance of role models and how you can use the question, "What would Batman do?" to help you be a Stoic.
- How Stoicism can help us build better relationships; and
- The very best 8 spiritual exercises that will create a Stoic in You

If you are tired of living life like you are always on the run and want to be able to increase your happiness, your contentment, and even your relationships—this guidebook has the answers for you.

It doesn't matter who you are right now, how many time you've felt guilty, how many failures you've experienced and how many times you've already tried to be a better person following this theory and that therapy. Stoicism has a really simple and practical approach that will guide you step-by-step to turn your life around by providing you with the right prospectives of the reality we live in.

So, make sure to check it out and learn how you can implement the ideas of Stoicism and all is philosophies into your life as well.

CLICK THE BUY BUTTON NOW!

www.ingramcontent.com/pod-product-compliance
Ingram Content Group UK Ltd.
Pitfield, Milton Keynes, MK11 3LW, UK
UKHW022226230426
12048UKWH00016BA/1081